IDEA® PICTURE DICTIONARY 1

An IDEA® Language Development Resource

Ballard & Tighe

Brea, California

Phonics Consultant

Dr. Norma Inabinette received her doctorate in education and psychology from the University of Buffalo. She is a professor emeritus at California State University, Fullerton. Her 27-year teaching career included a specialization in the diagnosis of reading disabilities and remedial instruction. She also directed the campus reading clinic, providing instruction to community members with reading disabilities. She currently conducts staff development and consults with school districts, publishers, and community agencies throughout Southern California.

Language Development Consultant

Bonnie McKenna received her teaching credential from the University of California, Riverside and her TESL certificate and CLAD credential from the University of California, Irvine. She has been an educator for more than 30 years, working as an elementary-level teacher, a college lecturer, and a teacher of adult ESL. She currently teaches and develops curriculum for the Community Based English Tutoring (CBET) program in the Capistrano Unified School District in California. She was one of the first teachers to pioneer the CBET program in 1999.

Reviewers

The *IDEA Picture Dictionary 1* greatly benefited from the educators who carefully reviewed the dictionary and provided helpful comments and suggestions.

Patricia Amaya-Thetford, Alcott Elementary School, Pomona, California
Gilda Bazan-Lopez, Educational Consultant, Houston, Texas
Beverly Crowe, Gallup-McKinley County Public Schools, Gallup, New Mexico
Gretchen Gross, Yuma District #1, Yuma, Arizona
Dr. Joyce Lancaster, Educational Consultant, Tampa, Florida
Robyn Ospital, La Habra City School District, La Habra, California
Dr. Betsy Rymes, University of Georgia, Athens, Georgia
Dr. Patricia Sanchez-Diaz, Parent Consultant, Menlo Park, California
Karen Shaw, Educational Consultant, Brea, California
Caryn Sonberg, Cora Kelly Magnet School, Alexandria, Virginia
Ann Stekelberg, Majestic Way Elementary School, San Jose, California
Dr. Connie Williams, Educational Consultant, Menlo Park, California

An IDEA® Language Development Resource

Managing Editor: Dr. Roberta Stathis
Second Edition Editor: Allison Mangrum
Editorial Staff: Kristin Belsher and Sean O'Brien
Program Consultants: Patrice Sonberg Gotsch and Jill Kinkade
Art Director: Liliana Cartelli
Desktop Publishing Coordinator: Kathleen Styffe
Printing Coordinator: Cathy Sanchez
Contributing Artists: Gina Capaldi, Sabrina Lammé, and Leilani Trollinger
Translators: Choice Translating and Interpreting, Inc.

2006 Printing
Revised Edition
ISBN 1-55501-523-9   Catalog #2-039

IDEA® Picture Dictionary 1

Contents

How to Use This

This shows **how to write** the letter.

These are **guide words**. Guide words tell you the first and last words defined on the page.

The words are in **ABC order**.

A B C D E F G H I J K L M N O P Q R S T U V W X Y Z

A a A a

airplane / ankle

airplane (AYR-playn)

Spanish: avión	**Pilipino:** eroplano
Vietnamese: phi cơ	**Chinese:** 飞机 / 飛機
Hmong: dav hlau	**French:** avion

alligator (AL-uh-gay-tur)

Spanish: cocodrilo	**Pilipino:** buwaya
Vietnamese: cá sấu	**Chinese:** 鳄鱼 / 鱷魚
Hmong: kheb	**French:** alligator

ambulance (AM-byoo-luns)

Spanish: ambulancia	**Pilipino:** ambulansiya
Vietnamese: xe cứu thương	**Chinese:** 救护车 / 救護車
Hmong: tsheb thauj mob	**French:** ambulance

animal (AN-ni-mul)

Spanish: animal	**Pilipino:** hayop
Vietnamese: thú vật	**Chinese:** 动物 / 動物
Hmong: tsiaj	**French:** animal

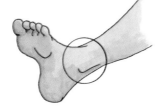

ankle (ANG-kul)

Spanish: tobillo	**Pilipino:** bukungbukong
Vietnamese: mắt cá chân	**Chinese:** 脚脖子,踝 / 腳踝
Hmong: pob taws	**French:** cheville

8

4

Dictionary

This is a **fun activity** for you to try.

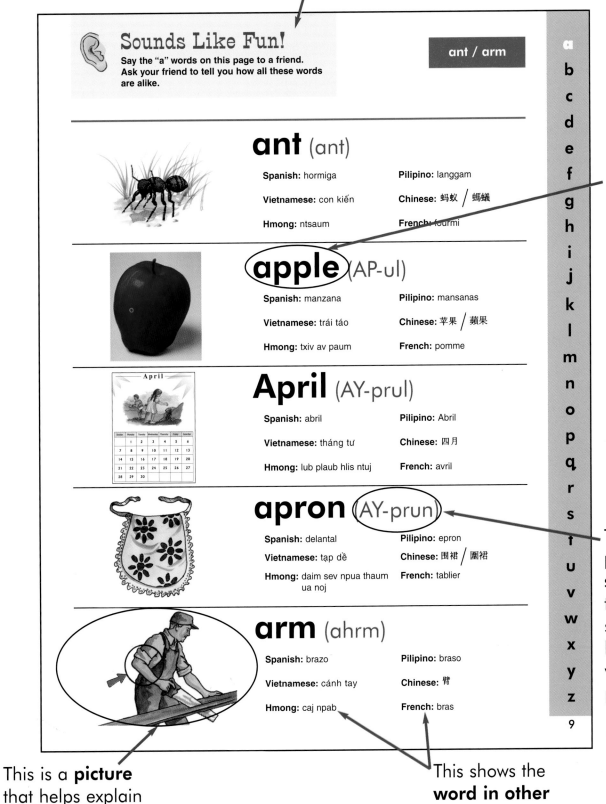

ant / arm

Sounds Like Fun!

Say the "a" words on this page to a friend. Ask your friend to tell you how all these words are alike.

ant (ant)

Spanish: hormiga
Pilipino: langgam
Vietnamese: con kiến
Chinese: 蚂蚁 / 螞蟻
Hmong: ntsaum
French: fourmi

apple (AP-ul)

This is a **word**.

Spanish: manzana
Pilipino: mansanas
Vietnamese: trái táo
Chinese: 苹果 / 蘋果
Hmong: txiv av paum
French: pomme

April (AY-prul)

Spanish: abril
Pilipino: Abril
Vietnamese: tháng tư
Chinese: 四月
Hmong: lub plaub hlis ntuj
French: avril

apron (AY-prun)

Spanish: delantal
Pilipino: epron
Vietnamese: tạp dề
Chinese: 围裙 / 圍裙
Hmong: daim sev npua thaum ua noj
French: tablier

arm (ahrm)

Spanish: brazo
Pilipino: braso
Vietnamese: cánh tay
Chinese: 臂
Hmong: caj npab
French: bras

a b c d e f g h i j k l m n o p q r s t u v w x y z

9

This is the **phonetic spelling** of the word. It shows you how to say the word. (See pages 6 and 7 for the Pronunciation Key.)

This is a **picture** that helps explain the word.

This shows the **word in other languages**.

5

Here's the Key!

Each dictionary has a guide or pronunciation key to help readers understand how to say words correctly. The pronunciation key for the *IDEA Picture Dictionary 1* appears below and on page 7. It is a phonetic pronunciation guide. This means that you can learn how to say a word by reading the sounds the letters make. Look at the example to see how this pronunciation key works.

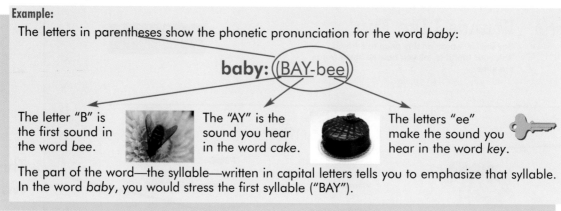

Example:

The letters in parentheses show the phonetic pronunciation for the word *baby*:

baby: (BAY-bee)

The letter "B" is the first sound in the word *bee*.

The "AY" is the sound you hear in the word *cake*.

The letters "ee" make the sound you hear in the word *key*.

The part of the word—the syllable—written in capital letters tells you to emphasize that syllable. In the word *baby*, you would stress the first syllable ("BAY").

Using this pronunciation key is an easy and fun way to learn how to pronounce words correctly. You can say all the words in this dictionary if you have the key!

VOWEL SOUNDS

A

SYMBOL	KEY WORDS
a	ant
ay	cake
ah	clock
aw	ball
ayr	hair

E

SYMBOL	KEY WORDS
e	bed
ee	key

I

SYMBOL	KEY WORDS
i	chick
iy	tiger

O

SYMBOL	KEY WORDS
oh	coat
oo	boot
oi	boy
ohr	door
ow	owl

U

SYMBOL	KEY WORDS
u	foot, bird
u	chicken
uh	bug
uh	kangaroo

International Phonetic Alphabet

ă	ant	ŏ	clock
ā	cake	ō	coat
âr	hair	ô	ball
ĕ	bed	o͝o	foot
ē	key	o͞o	boot
ĭ	chick	ou	owl
ī	tiger	ŭ	bug
oi	boy	ə	chicken; kangaroo

CONSONANT SOUNDS

SYMBOL	KEY WORDS		SYMBOL	KEY WORDS	
b	bee		r	roof	
ch	chin		s	saw	
d	doll		sh	sheep	
f	fish		t	toe	
g	goat		th	Thursday	
h	hat		th	mother	
j	juice		v	van	
k	cat		w	water	
l	lip		wh	white	
m	map		y	yellow	
n	nail		z	zebra	
ng	king		zh	television	
p	pail				

NOTE: The pronunciation key is derived from the following three sources: *American Heritage Dictionary of the English Language, 1981; Oxford American Dictionary: Heald Colleges Edition, 1982; Webster's New World College Dictionary, Third Edition, 1990.*

AaAa

airplane (AYR-playn)

Spanish: avión   **Pilipino:** eroplano

Vietnamese: phi cơ   **Chinese:** 飞机／飛機

Hmong: dav hlau   **French:** avion

alligator (AL-uh-gay-tur)

Spanish: cocodrilo   **Pilipino:** buwaya

Vietnamese: cá sấu   **Chinese:** 鳄鱼／鱷魚

Hmong: kheb   **French:** alligator

ambulance (AM-byoo-luns)

Spanish: ambulancia   **Pilipino:** ambulansiya

Vietnamese: xe cứu thương   **Chinese:** 救护车／救護車

Hmong: tsheb thauj mob   **French:** ambulance

animal (AN-ni-mul)

Spanish: animal   **Pilipino:** hayop

Vietnamese: thú vật   **Chinese:** 动物／動物

Hmong: tsiaj   **French:** animal

ankle (ANG-kul)

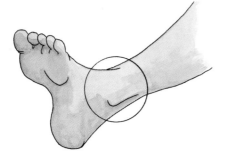

Spanish: tobillo   **Pilipino:** bukungbukong

Vietnamese: mắt cá chân   **Chinese:** 脚脖子,踝／腳踝

Hmong: pob taws   **French:** cheville

Sounds Like Fun!

Say the "a" words on this page to a friend.
Ask your friend to tell you how all these words
are alike.

ant (ant)

Spanish: hormiga

Vietnamese: con kiến

Hmong: ntsaum

Pilipino: langgam

Chinese: 蚂蚁 / 螞蟻

French: fourmi

apple (AP-ul)

Spanish: manzana

Vietnamese: trái táo

Hmong: txiv av paum

Pilipino: mansanas

Chinese: 苹果 / 蘋果

French: pomme

April (AY-prul)

Spanish: abril

Vietnamese: tháng tư

Hmong: lub plaub hlis ntuj

Pilipino: Abril

Chinese: 四月

French: avril

apron (AY-prun)

Spanish: delantal

Vietnamese: tạp dề

Hmong: daim sev npua thaum
ua noj

Pilipino: epron

Chinese: 围裙 / 圍裙

French: tablier

arm (ahrm)

Spanish: brazo

Vietnamese: cánh tay

Hmong: caj npab

Pilipino: braso

Chinese: 臂

French: bras

a
b
c
d
e
f
g
h
i
j
k
l
m
n
o
p
q
r
s
t
u
v
w
x
y
z

artist (AHR-tist)

Spanish: artista

Vietnamese: họa sĩ

Hmong: neeg kos duab

Pilipino: pintor

Chinese: 艺术家／藝術家

French: artiste

astronaut (AS-truh-naht)

Spanish: astronauta

Vietnamese: phi hành gia

Hmong: tus neeg mus saum qaum ntuj

Pilipino: astronaut, astronot, astronawt

Chinese: 宇航员／太空人

French: astronaute

August (AH-gust)

Spanish: agosto

Vietnamese: tháng tám

Hmong: lub yim hli ntlub yim hli ntuj

Pilipino: Agosto

Chinese: 八月

French: août

aunt (ant)

Spanish: tía

Vietnamese: cô, dì

Hmong: phauj, niam tais hlob, niam tais laus, niam dab laug, niam hlob, niam ntxawm

Pilipino: tita

Chinese: 伯母,叔母,姑妈,姨妈／伯母,叔母,姑媽,姨媽

French: tante

axe (aks)

Spanish: hacha

Vietnamese: cái rìu

Hmong: rab taus

Pilipino: palakol

Chinese: 斧

French: hache

Bb Bb

baby (BAY-bee)

Spanish: bebé
Pilipino: sanggol
Vietnamese: em bé
Chinese: 婴儿 / 嬰兒
Hmong: me nyuam mos liab
French: bébé

back (bak)

Spanish: espalda
Pilipino: likod
Vietnamese: cái lưng
Chinese: 背
Hmong: nrob qaum
French: dos

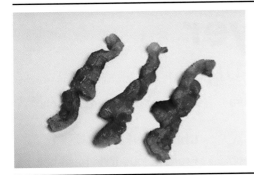

bacon (BAY-kun)

Spanish: tocino
Pilipino: bacon
Vietnamese: thịt mỡ muối
Chinese: 熏肉 / 培根
Hmong: nqaij sawb
French: lard, bacon

badge (baj)

Spanish: insignia
Pilipino: tsapa
Vietnamese: huy hiệu
Chinese: 徽章
Hmong: daim ntawv coj qhia npe
French: insigne

baker (BAY-kur)

Spanish: panadera / panadero
Pilipino: panadero
Vietnamese: người nướng bánh
Chinese: 面包师 / 烤麵包師
Hmong: tus neeg ci mov mog thiab mov mog ncu
French: boulangère / boulanger

a b c d e f g h i j k l m n o p q r s t u v w x y z

11

A
B
C
D
E
F
G
H
I
J
K
L
M
N
O
P
Q
R
S
T
U
V
W
X
Y
Z

12

ball (bawl)

Spanish: bola, pelota, balón   **Pilipino:** bola

Vietnamese: trái banh   **Chinese:** 球

Hmong: lub pob   **French:** balle

balloon (bu-LOON)

Spanish: globo   **Pilipino:** lobo

Vietnamese: bong bóng   **Chinese:** 汽球

Hmong: zais   **French:** ballon

ballplayer (BAWL-play-ur)

Spanish: jugador / jugadora de pelota   **Pilipino:** manlalaro ng bola

Vietnamese: cầu thủ   **Chinese:** 球员／球員

Hmong: tus neeg ntaus pob   **French:** joueur de base-ball

banana (bu-NAN-uh)

Spanish: plátano, banano   **Pilipino:** saging

Vietnamese: trái chuối   **Chinese:** 香蕉

Hmong: txiv tsawb   **French:** banane

bank teller (bangk TEL-ur)

Spanish: cajera / cajero   **Pilipino:** teler

Vietnamese: thu ngân viên tại ngân hàng   **Chinese:** 银行出纳员／銀行出納員

Hmong: tus pauv nyiaj   **French:** caissière / caissier

barber (BAHR-bur)

Spanish: peluquero / peluquera   **Pilipino:** barbero

Vietnamese: thợ hớt tóc   **Chinese:** 理发师 / 理髮師

Hmong: kws txiav plaub hau   **French:** coiffeur pour hommes

barn (bahrn)

Spanish: granero   **Pilipino:** kamalig

Vietnamese: kho vựa chứa nông sản và gia súc   **Chinese:** 谷仓 / 穀倉

Hmong: lub txhab   **French:** grange

bars (bahrz)

Spanish: barras   **Pilipino:** baras

Vietnamese: xà ngang   **Chinese:** 杠杆 / 槓桿

Hmong: kav hlau   **French:** barres

baseball (BAYS-bawl)

Spanish: béisbol   **Pilipino:** baseball

Vietnamese: dã cầu   **Chinese:** 棒球

Hmong: lub pob cuam   **French:** base-ball

bat (bat)

Spanish: bate   **Pilipino:** bat

Vietnamese: gậy đánh bóng chày   **Chinese:** 球棒

Hmong: qws ntaus pob   **French:** batte

a
b
c
d
e
f
g
h
i
j
k
l
m
n
o
p
q
r
s
t
u
v
w
x
y
z

bat (bat)

Spanish: murciélago

Pilipino: paniki

Vietnamese: con dơi

Chinese: 蝙蝠

Hmong: puav

French: chauve-souris

bathing suit
(BAY-thing soot)

Spanish: ropa de baño

Pilipino: damit panligo

Vietnamese: quần áo tắm

Chinese: 游泳衣

Hmong: khaub ncaws da dej

French: maillot de bain

bathroom (BATH-room)

Spanish: cuarto de baño

Pilipino: banyo

Vietnamese: phòng tắm

Chinese: 浴室

Hmong: chav dej

French: salle de bains

bathtub (BATH-tuhb)

Spanish: bañera

Pilipino: bathtub

Vietnamese: bồn tắm

Chinese: 浴缸

Hmong: dab da dej

French: baignoire

bean (been)

Spanish: haba, frijol

Pilipino: bins

Vietnamese: đậu

Chinese: 豆

Hmong: taum

French: haricot

Sounds Like Fun!

Think of three things that start with the /b/ sound that you like to play with. Ask a partner to guess what the things are.

bear (bayr)

Spanish: oso

Vietnamese: con gấu

Hmong: dais

Pilipino: oso

Chinese: 熊

French: ours

beaver (BEE-vur)

Spanish: castor

Vietnamese: con hải ly

Hmong: nas kos dej

Pilipino: beaver

Chinese: 海狸

French: castor

bed (bed)

Spanish: cama

Vietnamese: cái giường

Hmong: txaj

Pilipino: kama

Chinese: 床

French: lit

bedroom (BED-room)

Spanish: dormitorio

Vietnamese: phòng ngủ

Hmong: chav pw

Pilipino: silid-tulugan

Chinese: 寢室 / 寝室

French: chambre à coucher

bee (bee)

Spanish: abeja

Vietnamese: con ong

Hmong: muv

Pilipino: bubuyog

Chinese: 蜜蜂

French: abeille

a **b** c d e f g h i j k l m n o p q r s t u v w x y z

A B C D E F G H I J K L M N O P Q R S T U V W X Y Z

belt (belt)

Spanish: cinturón

Pilipino: sinturon

Vietnamese: dây nịt

Chinese: 皮带 / 皮帶

Hmong: txoj siv tawv

French: ceinture

bench (bench)

Spanish: banco

Pilipino: bangko

Vietnamese: ghế dài

Chinese: 板凳

Hmong: lub rooj zaum

French: banc

bicycle (BIY-sik-ul)

Spanish: bicicleta

Pilipino: bisikleta

Vietnamese: xe đạp

Chinese: 脚踏车 / 腳踏車

Hmong: tsheb kauj vab

French: bicyclette

bird (burd)

Spanish: pájaro

Pilipino: ibon

Vietnamese: con chim

Chinese: 鸟 / 鳥

Hmong: noog

French: oiseau

birthday (BURTH-day)

Spanish: cumpleaños

Pilipino: kaarawan

Vietnamese: sinh nhật

Chinese: 生日

Hmong: hnub yug

French: anniversaire

black (blak)

Spanish: negro

Pilipino: itim

Vietnamese: màu đen

Chinese: 黑

Hmong: dub

French: noir / noire

block (blahk)

Spanish: bloque

Pilipino: bloke

Vietnamese: khối gỗ

Chinese: 积木 / 積木

Hmong: thawv ua si

French: bloc

blouse (blows)

Spanish: blusa

Pilipino: blusa

Vietnamese: áo sơ-mi đàn bà

Chinese: 上衫 / 上衣

Hmong: tsho poj niam

French: corsage, chemisier

blue (bloo)

Spanish: azul

Pilipino: asul

Vietnamese: màu xanh

Chinese: 蓝 / 藍

Hmong: xiav

French: bleu / bleue

body (BAHD-ee)

Spanish: cuerpo

Pilipino: katawan

Vietnamese: cơ thể

Chinese: 身体 / 身體

Hmong: lub cev

French: corps

a b c d e f g h i j k l m n o p q r s t u v w x y z

A
B
C
D
E
F
G
H
I
J
K
L
M
N
O
P
Q
R
S
T
U
V
W
X
Y
Z

book (buk)

Spanish: libro

Pilipino: libro

Vietnamese: cuốn sách

Chinese: 书／書

Hmong: phau ntawv

French: livre

boot (boot)

Spanish: bota

Pilipino: bota

Vietnamese: giày ống

Chinese: 靴

Hmong: khau tawv looj

French: botte

bow and arrow
(boh and AYR-oh)

Spanish: arco y flecha

Pilipino: pana

Vietnamese: cung và tên

Chinese: 弓 和 箭

Hmong: hneev nti thiab xib xub

French: arc et flèche

bowl (bohl)

Spanish: bol

Pilipino: mangkok

Vietnamese: cái chén

Chinese: 碗

Hmong: tais

French: bol

boxer (BAHK-sur)

Spanish: boxeador / boxeadora

Pilipino: boksingero

Vietnamese: võ sĩ quyền anh

Chinese: 拳师／拳師

Hmong: tus neeg ntaus nrig

French: boxeur / boxeuse

boy (boi)

Spanish: muchacho

Vietnamese: bé trai

Hmong: tus tub

Pilipino: batang lalaki

Chinese: 男孩

French: garçon

bracelet (BRAYS-lit)

Spanish: brazalete

Vietnamese: vòng đeo tay

Hmong: saw tes

Pilipino: pulseras

Chinese: 手镯 / 手鐲

French: bracelet

bread (bred)

Spanish: pan

Vietnamese: bánh mì

Hmong: mov mog ncu

Pilipino: tinapay

Chinese: 面包 / 麵包

French: pain

breakfast (BREK-fust)

Spanish: desayuno

Vietnamese: bữa ăn sáng

Hmong: tshais

Pilipino: almusal

Chinese: 早餐

French: petit déjeuner

bridge (brij)

Spanish: puente

Vietnamese: cây cầu

Hmong: choj

Pilipino: tulay

Chinese: 桥 / 橋

French: pont

a
b
c
d
e
f
g
h
i
j
k
l
m
n
o
p
q
r
s
t
u
v
w
x
y
z

Dictionary Detective

Brown is a color. Find two other "b" words in this book that are colors.

broom (broom)

Spanish: escoba   **Pilipino:** walis

Vietnamese: cái chổi   **Chinese:** 扫帚 / 掃帚

Hmong: khaub ruab   **French:** balai

brother (BRUHTH-ur)

Spanish: hermano   **Pilipino:** kapatid na lalaki

Vietnamese: anh, em   **Chinese:** 兄弟

Hmong: tij laug, kwv, nus   **French:** frère

brown (brown)

Spanish: marrón   **Pilipino:** brown

Vietnamese: màu nâu   **Chinese:** 褐色

Hmong: yeeb yuj xem   **French:** marron

brush (bruhsh)

Spanish: escobilla   **Pilipino:** escoba

Vietnamese: bàn chải   **Chinese:** 刷

Hmong: khaub ruab   **French:** brosse

bucket (BUHK-it)

Spanish: cubo   **Pilipino:** timba

Vietnamese: cái xô   **Chinese:** 桶

Hmong: thoob   **French:** seau

A B C D E F G H I J K L M N O P Q R S T U V W X Y Z

buffalo (BUHF-uh-loh)

Spanish: búfalo

Pilipino: bupalo

Vietnamese: con bò rừng

Chinese: 水牛

Hmong: nyuj qus

French: buffle

bug (buhg)

Spanish: bicho

Pilipino: kulisap

Vietnamese: con bọ, côn trùng

Chinese: 虫／蟲

Hmong: kab

French: punaise

bulletin board (BUL-uh-tun bohrd)

Spanish: tablero de anuncios

Pilipino: bulletin board

Vietnamese: bảng thông báo

Chinese: 布告牌／公告欄

Hmong: daim ntoo lo ntawv

French: tableau d'affichage

bus (buhs)

Spanish: autobús

Pilipino: bus

Vietnamese: xe buýt

Chinese: 公车／公車

Hmong: npav

French: autobus

bus driver (buhs DRIY-vur)

Spanish: conductora / conductor del autobús

Pilipino: tsuper ng bus

Vietnamese: tài xế xe buýt

Chinese: 公车司机／公車司機

Hmong: tus tsav npav

French: conducteur d'autobus

bush (bush)

Spanish: arbusto

Pilipino: palumpong

Vietnamese: bụi cây

Chinese: 灌木

Hmong: nroj tsuag

French: buisson

butcher (BUCH-ur)

Spanish: carnicero / carnicera

Pilipino: matadero

Vietnamese: người hàng thịt

Chinese: 肉販 / 肉販

Hmong: tus neeg tua tsiaj thiab muag nqaij

French: boucher / bouchère

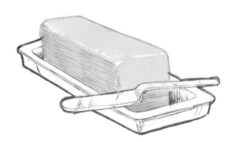

butter (BUHT-ur)

Spanish: mantequilla

Pilipino: mantikilya

Vietnamese: bơ

Chinese: 黃油 / 奶油, 牛油

Hmong: npaws

French: beurre

butterfly (BUHT-ur-fliy)

Spanish: mariposa

Pilipino: paruparo

Vietnamese: con bướm

Chinese: 蝴蝶

Hmong: npauj npaim

French: papillon

cafeteria
(kaf-uh-TEER-ee-uh)

Spanish: cafetería

Vietnamese: quán ăn tự dọn

Hmong: chav noj mov

Pilipino: kapeteriya

Chinese: 自助餐馆 / 自助餐館

French: cafétéria

cake (kayk)

Spanish: pastel

Vietnamese: bánh ngọt

Hmong: khej, ncuav qab zib

Pilipino: keyk

Chinese: 蛋糕

French: gâteau

calendar (KAL-uhn-dur)

Spanish: calendario

Vietnamese: lịch

Hmong: ntawv saib hnub nyoog

Pilipino: kalendaryo

Chinese: 历 / 曆

French: calendrier

calf (kaf)

Spanish: becerro

Vietnamese: con bê

Hmong: me nyuam nyuj

Pilipino: guya

Chinese: 小牛

French: veau

camel (KAM-ul)

Spanish: camello

Vietnamese: con lạc đà

Hmong: nees daj dua

Pilipino: kamelyo

Chinese: 骆驼 / 駱駝

French: chameau

a
b
c
d
e
f
g
h
i
j
k
l
m
n
o
p
q
r
s
t
u
v
w
x
y
z

camper (KAM-pur)

Spanish: vehículo de remolque para acampar
Pilipino: kamper
Vietnamese: xe cắm trại
Chinese: 露营车 / 露營車
Hmong: lub tsev txawb saum tsheb
French: camping-car

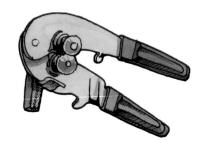

can opener (kan OH-puhn-ur)

Spanish: abrelatas
Pilipino: abrelata
Vietnamese: cái khui đồ hộp
Chinese: 罐头启子 / 開罐器
Hmong: tus tho kaus poom
French: ouvre-boîte

canoe (kuh-NOO)

Spanish: canoa
Pilipino: banka
Vietnamese: thuyền độc mộc
Chinese: 独木舟 / 獨木舟
Hmong: nkoj txeeb kab
French: canoë

car (kahr)

Spanish: carro, auto
Pilipino: kotse
Vietnamese: xe
Chinese: 车 / 車
Hmong: tsheb
French: voiture

carpenter (KAHR-puhn-tur)

Spanish: carpintero / carpintera
Pilipino: karpintero
Vietnamese: thợ mộc
Chinese: 木匠
Hmong: neeg ua tsev
French: charpentier / menuisier

A B C D E F G H I J K L M N O P Q R S T U V W X Y Z

Sounds Like Fun!

Change the first letter in the word *cat* to make new words. How many new words did you make?

carrot (KAYR-ut)

Spanish: zanahoria	**Pilipino:** karot
Vietnamese: củ cà rốt	**Chinese:** 葫萝卜 / 胡蘿蔔
Hmong: qos hmab ntug	**French:** carotte

cat (kat)

Spanish: gato	**Pilipino:** pusa
Vietnamese: con mèo	**Chinese:** 猫 / 貓
Hmong: miv	**French:** chat / chatte

caterpillar (KAT-ur-pil-ur)

Spanish: oruga	**Pilipino:** higad
Vietnamese: sâu bướm	**Chinese:** 毛虫 / 毛毛蟲
Hmong: kab nyuam dev	**French:** chenille

CD (SEE-DEE)

Spanish: CD	**Pilipino:** CD
Vietnamese: đĩa CD	**Chinese:** 光盘 / 光碟
Hmong: daim CD	**French:** CD

CD player (SEE-DEE PLAY-ur)

Spanish: lector de CD	**Pilipino:** CD player
Vietnamese: máy CD	**Chinese:** 光盘播放机 / 光碟播放機
Hmong: lub tshuab tso daim CD mloog	**French:** lecteur de CD

a
b
c
d
e
f
g
h
i
j
k
l
m
n
o
p
q
r
s
t
u
v
w
x
y
z

25

cheek (cheek)

Spanish: mejilla　　**Pilipino:** pisngi

Vietnamese: cái má　　**Chinese:** 颊 / 頰

Hmong: plhu　　**French:** joue

cheese (cheez)

Spanish: queso　　**Pilipino:** keso

Vietnamese: phó mát　　**Chinese:** 奶酪

Hmong: tshij　　**French:** fromage

chemist (KEM-ist)

Spanish: química / químico　　**Pilipino:** kimiko

Vietnamese: nhà hoá học　　**Chinese:** 化学家 / 化學家

Hmong: tus tov tshuaj　　**French:** chimiste

cherry (CHAYR-ee)

Spanish: cereza　　**Pilipino:** seresa

Vietnamese: anh đào　　**Chinese:** 櫻桃 / 櫻桃

Hmong: txiv ntoo qab zib　　**French:** cerise

chest of drawers
(chest uv drohrz)

Spanish: cómoda　　**Pilipino:** aparador

Vietnamese: tủ có ngăn kéo　　**Chinese:** (带抽屉的)衣橱 / 帶抽屜的衣橱

Hmong: tub rau khaub ncaws　　**French:** commode

Sounds Like Fun!

Take "ch" away from *chin*. Then put each letter of the alphabet in front of "_in." Did you make any real words? What were they?

chick (chik)

Spanish: pollito

Vietnamese: con gà con

Hmong: me nyuam qaib

Pilipino: sisiw

Chinese: 小鸡 / 小雞

French: poussin

chicken (CHIK-un)

Spanish: pollo

Vietnamese: con gà

Hmong: qaib

Pilipino: manok

Chinese: 鸡 / 雞

French: poulet

child (chiyld)

Spanish: niña / niño

Vietnamese: trẻ em

Hmong: me nyuam

Pilipino: bata

Chinese: 小孩

French: enfant

chimney (CHIM-nee)

Spanish: chimenea

Vietnamese: ống khói

Hmong: qhov raj cua

Pilipino: tsiminea

Chinese: 烟囱 / 煙囱

French: cheminée

chin (chin)

Spanish: barbilla, mentón

Vietnamese: cái cằm

Hmong: pob tsaig

Pilipino: baba

Chinese: 下巴

French: menton

a b c d e f g h i j k l m n o p q r s t u v w x y z

29

A
B
C
D
E
F
G
H
I
J
K
L
M
N
O
P
Q
R
S
T
U
V
W
X
Y
Z

chipmunk (CHIP-munk)

Spanish: ardilla listada   **Pilipino:** chipmunk

Vietnamese: con sóc chuột   **Chinese:** 花栗鼠

Hmong: nas ciav   **French:** tamia

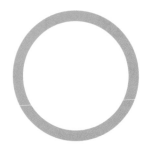

circle (SUR-kul)

Spanish: círculo   **Pilipino:** bilog

Vietnamese: vòng tròn   **Chinese:** 圆 / 圓

Hmong: voj voog   **French:** cercle

city (SIT-ee)

Spanish: ciudad   **Pilipino:** siyudad

Vietnamese: thành phố   **Chinese:** 城市 / 城市

Hmong: lub zos   **French:** ville

clock (klahk)

Spanish: reloj   **Pilipino:** orasan

Vietnamese: đồng hồ   **Chinese:** 钟 / 鐘

Hmong: lub thaus   **French:** horloge

closet (KLAHZ-it)

Spanish: armario, ropero   **Pilipino:** kloset

Vietnamese: cái tủ   **Chinese:** 壁橱

Hmong: kem tsev rau khoom   **French:** placard

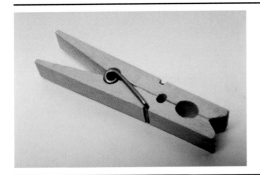

clothesline (KLOHZ-liyn)

Spanish: tendedero   **Pilipino:** sampayan

Vietnamese: dây phơi quần áo   **Chinese:** 晒衣绳 / 曬衣繩

Hmong: hlua ziab khaub ncaws   **French:** corde à linge

clothespin (KLOHZ-pin)

Spanish: pinza para tender ropa   **Pilipino:** sipit

Vietnamese: kẹp phơi quần áo   **Chinese:** 衣服夹 / 衣服夾

Hmong: pas tais khaub ncaws   **French:** pince à linge

clown (klown)

Spanish: payaso   **Pilipino:** payaso

Vietnamese: tên hề   **Chinese:** 小丑

Hmong: neeg zab   **French:** clown

coat (koht)

Spanish: chaqueta   **Pilipino:** abrigo

Vietnamese: áo ngoài   **Chinese:** 外套

Hmong: tsho tiv no   **French:** manteau

coffee maker
(KAW-fee MAY-kur)

Spanish: máquina de café   **Pilipino:** panggawa ng kape

Vietnamese: máy pha cà phê   **Chinese:** 咖啡器

Hmong: lub ua kas fes   **French:** cafetière électrique

a b c d e f g h i j k l m n o p q r s t u v w x y z

31

A
B
c
D
E
F
G
H
I
J
K
L
M
N
O
P
Q
R
S
T
U
V
W
X
Y
Z

coffeepot (KAW-fee-paht)

Spanish: cafetera   **Pilipino:** takore

Vietnamese: bình cà phê   **Chinese:** 咖啡壶 / 咖啡壺

Hmong: lub rhaub kas fes   **French:** cafetière

colt (kohlt)

Spanish: potro   **Pilipino:** potro

Vietnamese: ngựa đực con   **Chinese:** 小马 / 小馬

Hmong: me nyuam nees   **French:** poulain

comb (kohm)

Spanish: peine   **Pilipino:** suklay

Vietnamese: cái lược   **Chinese:** 梳子

Hmong: zuag   **French:** peigne

compass (KUHM-pus)

Spanish: brújula   **Pilipino:** kompas

Vietnamese: địa bàn   **Chinese:** 罗盘 / 指南針

Hmong: cwj cim seem   **French:** compas

computer (kuhm-PYOO-tur)

Spanish: computadora, ordenador   **Pilipino:** kompyuter

Vietnamese: máy điện toán   **Chinese:** 电子计算机 / 電腦

Hmong: kaib lawj ceem   **French:** ordinateur

Dictionary Detective

Find the word in this book that begins with the letter m and ends with the letter c. What word is it?

container (kuhn-TAY-nur)

Spanish: recipiente

Vietnamese: vật đựng

Hmong: taub ntim khoom, kua

Pilipino: lalagyan

Chinese: 容器 / 容器

French: container, conteneur, récipient

cook (kuk)

Spanish: cocinero / cocinera

Vietnamese: người đầu bếp

Hmong: tus ua zaub mov

Pilipino: kusinero

Chinese: 厨师 / 厨師

French: cuisinier / cuisinière

cookie (KUK-ee)

Spanish: galleta

Vietnamese: bánh bít-qui ngọt

Hmong: mov mog

Pilipino: cookie

Chinese: 饼乾 / 餅乾

French: biscuit

corn (kohrn)

Spanish: maíz

Vietnamese: bắp

Hmong: pob kws

Pilipino: mais

Chinese: 玉蜀黍

French: maïs

cottage cheese (KAHT-ij cheez)

Spanish: requesón

Vietnamese: phó mát trắng

Hmong: tshij dawb

Pilipino: kesong puti

Chinese: 农家奶酪 / 農家奶酪

French: fromage blanc

a b **c** d e f g h i j k l m n o p q r s t u v w x y z

A B **C** D E F G H I J K L M N O P Q R S T U V W X Y Z

cupcake (KUHP-kayk)

Spanish: pastelito

Pilipino: kapkeyk

Vietnamese: bánh nướng hình tách

Chinese: 杯形饼 / 杯形餅

Hmong: mov mog khob

French: petit gâteau

curve (kurv)

Spanish: curva

Pilipino: kurba

Vietnamese: đường cong

Chinese: 弯 / 彎

Hmong: nkhaus

French: courbe

custodian (kuhs-TOH-dee-un)

Spanish: guardián / guardiana

Pilipino: diyanitor

Vietnamese: người lao công

Chinese: 清洁工 / 清潔工

Hmong: tus tu tsev

French: gardien / gardienne

Dd

dancer (DANS-ur)

Spanish: bailarina / bailarín

Vietnamese: vũ công

Hmong: tus neeg seev cev

Pilipino: mananayaw

Chinese: 舞蹈家

French: danseuse / danseur

December (di-SEM-bur)

Spanish: diciembre

Vietnamese: tháng chạp, tháng mười hai

Hmong: lub kaum ob hlis ntuj

Pilipino: Disyembre

Chinese: 十二月

French: décembre

deer (deer)

Spanish: ciervo, venado

Vietnamese: con nai

Hmong: mos lwj

Pilipino: usa

Chinese: 鹿

French: cerf

den (den)

Spanish: estudio

Vietnamese: phòng riêng nhỏ

Hmong: ib chav nyob los sis saib ntawv

Pilipino: den

Chinese: 小房

French: salon

dentist (DEN-tist)

Spanish: dentista

Vietnamese: nha sĩ

Hmong: kws kho hniav

Pilipino: dentista

Chinese: 牙医／牙醫

French: dentiste

a b c **d** e f g h i j k l m n o p q r s t u v w x y z

A
B
C
D
E
F
G
H
I
J
K
L
M
N
O
P
Q
R
S
T
U
V
W
X
Y
Z

Dictionary Detective

The guide words on this page are *desk* and *dining room*. What page number has the guide words *hat* and *helicopter*?

desk (desk)

Spanish: escritorio   **Pilipino:** desk

Vietnamese: cái bàn   **Chinese:** 桌子

Hmong: rooj sau ntawv   **French:** bureau

diamond (DIY-mund)

Spanish: diamante   **Pilipino:** diyamante

Vietnamese: hình thoi   **Chinese:** 钻石 / 鑽石

Hmong: lub pob ze diamond   **French:** losange

diaper (DIY-pur)

Spanish: pañal   **Pilipino:** lampin

Vietnamese: tả lót   **Chinese:** 尿布

Hmong: daiv pawm   **French:** couche

dime (diym)

Spanish: moneda de diez centavos   **Pilipino:** sampung sentimo

Vietnamese: đồng mười xu   **Chinese:** 一角

Hmong: kaum xees   **French:** pièce de 10 cents

dining room (DIYN-ing room)

Spanish: comedor   **Pilipino:** silid kainan

Vietnamese: phòng ăn   **Chinese:** 饭厅 / 飯廳

Hmong: chav noj mov   **French:** salle à manger

dinner (DIN-ur)

Spanish: cena

Pilipino: hapunan

Vietnamese: bữa ăn tối

Chinese: 晚餐

Hmong: hmo

French: dîner

dinosaur (DIY-nuh-sohr)

Spanish: dinosaurio

Pilipino: dinosaur

Vietnamese: con khủng long

Chinese: 恐龙 / 恐龍

Hmong: tsiaj loj txheej thaum ub

French: dinosaure

dish (dish)

Spanish: plato

Pilipino: pinggan

Vietnamese: cái dĩa

Chinese: 盘子 / 盤子

Hmong: tais diav

French: plat

dishpan (DISH-pan)

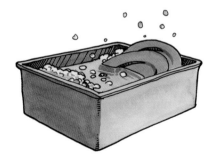

Spanish: fregadero

Pilipino: hugasan

Vietnamese: bồn rửa chén dĩa

Chinese: 洗碟用盆子 / 洗碗槽

Hmong: lub thoob rau tais diav

French: bassine

diskette (dis-KET)

Spanish: disquete

Pilipino: diskett

Vietnamese: dĩa từ

Chinese: 磁盘, 磁碟 / 磁碟片

Hmong: daim tsheej

French: disquette

a b c **d** e f g h i j k l m n o p q r s t u v w x y z

39

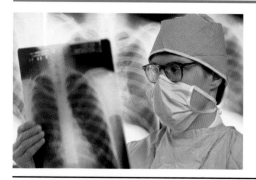

doctor (DAHK-tur)

Spanish: médico / médica   **Pilipino:** doktor

Vietnamese: bác sĩ   **Chinese:** 医师 / 醫師, 醫生

Hmong: kws kho mob   **French:** docteur

dog (dawg)

Spanish: perro   **Pilipino:** aso

Vietnamese: con chó   **Chinese:** 狗

Hmong: aub, dev   **French:** chien

doll (dahl)

Spanish: muñeca   **Pilipino:** manyika

Vietnamese: búp bê   **Chinese:** 玩偶

Hmong: me nyuam roj hmab   **French:** poupée

dollar bill (DAHL-ur bil)

Spanish: billete de dólar   **Pilipino:** isang dolyar

Vietnamese: tờ giấy bạc   **Chinese:** 一元纸钞 / 一元紙鈔

Hmong: nyiaj duas las   **French:** billet d'un dollar

dollhouse (DAHL-hows)

Spanish: casa de muñecas   **Pilipino:** bahay-bayahan

Vietnamese: nhà búp bê   **Chinese:** 玩偶屋

Hmong: tsev ua si rau me nyuam roj hmab   **French:** maison de poupée

dolphin (DAHL-fin)

Spanish: delfín **Pilipino:** dolpin

Vietnamese: cá heo **Chinese:** 海豚

Hmong: ntxhuab deg **French:** dauphin

door (dohr)

Spanish: puerta **Pilipino:** pintuan

Vietnamese: cửa ra vào **Chinese:** 门 / 門

Hmong: qhov rooj **French:** porte

dot (daht)

Spanish: punto **Pilipino:** tuldok

Vietnamese: dấu chấm **Chinese:** 点 / 點

Hmong: ib tee **French:** point

doughnut (DOH-nut)

Spanish: donut **Pilipino:** donat

Vietnamese: bánh ngọt đô nất **Chinese:** 面包圈 / 甜甜圈

Hmong: mov mog qab zib **French:** beignet

dress (dres)

Spanish: vestido **Pilipino:** bestida

Vietnamese: áo đầm **Chinese:** 洋装 / 洋裝

Hmong: tiab txuas tsho **French:** robe

a
b
c
d
e
f
g
h
i
j
k
l
m
n
o
p
q
r
s
t
u
v
w
x
y
z

A
B
C
D
E
F
G
H
I
J
K
L
M
N
O
P
Q
R
S
T
U
V
W
X
Y
Z

dressmaker
(DRES-may-kur)

Spanish: costurera

Pilipino: mananahi

Vietnamese: thợ may áo quần phụ nữ

Chinese: 女装裁缝师 / 女裝裁縫師

Hmong: tus neeg xaw tiab

French: couturière

drinking fountain
(DRINK-ing FOWN-tun)

Spanish: fuente de agua potable

Pilipino: inuman ng tubig

Vietnamese: vòi nước uống

Chinese: 饮水器 / 飲水機

Hmong: tus kais haus dej

French: fontaine d'eau potable

drum (druhm)

Spanish: tambor

Pilipino: tambol

Vietnamese: cái trống

Chinese: 鼓

Hmong: nruas

French: tambour

duck (duhk)

Spanish: pato

Pilipino: pato

Vietnamese: con vịt

Chinese: 鸭 / 鴨

Hmong: os

French: canard / cane

dustpan (DUHST-pan)

Spanish: recogedor

Pilipino: daspan

Vietnamese: cái hốt rác

Chinese: 簸箕 / 畚箕

Hmong: cib laug

French: pelle à poussière

DVD player
(DEE VEE DEE PLAY-ur)

Spanish: lector de DVD

Vietnamese: máy chơi DVD

Hmong: lub tshuab tso DVD saib los sis mloog

Pilipino: DVD player

Chinese: DVD 播放机／
DVD 播放機

French: lecteur de DVD

E e E e

A B C D **E** F G H I J K L M N O P Q R S T U V W X Y Z

eagle (EE-gul)

Spanish: águila
Pilipino: agila
Vietnamese: con chim ó
Chinese: 鷹 / 鷹
Hmong: dav
French: aigle

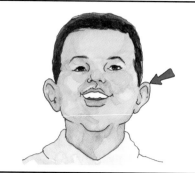

ear (eer)

Spanish: oreja
Pilipino: tenga
Vietnamese: cái tai
Chinese: 耳
Hmong: pob ntseg
French: oreille

egg (eg)

Spanish: huevo
Pilipino: itlog
Vietnamese: quả trứng
Chinese: 蛋
Hmong: qe
French: oeuf

eight (ayt)

8

eight pennies

Spanish: ocho
Pilipino: walo
Vietnamese: tám
Chinese: 八
Hmong: yim
French: huit

eighteen (ay-TEEN)

18

eighteen snails

Spanish: dieciocho
Pilipino: labingwalo
Vietnamese: mười tám
Chinese: 十八
Hmong: kaum yim
French: dix-huit

eighth (ayth)

Spanish: octavo

Pilipino: pangwalo

Vietnamese: thứ tám

Chinese: 第八

Hmong: zus yim

French: huitième

80

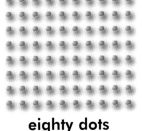

eighty dots

eighty (AY-tee)

Spanish: ochenta

Pilipino: walumpu

Vietnamese: tám mươi

Chinese: 八十

Hmong: yim caum

French: quatre-vingts

elbow (EL-boh)

Spanish: codo

Pilipino: siko

Vietnamese: khuỷu tay

Chinese: 肘

Hmong: luj tshib

French: coude

electrician (i-lek-TRISH-un)

Spanish: electricista

Pilipino: elektrisyan

Vietnamese: thợ điện

Chinese: 电气技师／電氣技師

Hmong: tus kho hluav taws xob

French: électricien

elephant (EL-uh-funt)

Spanish: elefante

Pilipino: elepante

Vietnamese: con voi

Chinese: 象

Hmong: ntxhw

French: éléphant

a
b
c
d
e
f
g
h
i
j
k
l
m
n
o
p
q
r
s
t
u
v
w
x
y
z

45

Sounds Like Fun!

Read the words on this page and clap as you say each syllable. How many words have only one syllable? Two syllables? Three syllables?

11

eleven caterpillars

eleven (i-LEV-un)

Spanish: once

Pilipino: labing-isa

Vietnamese: mười một

Chinese: 十一

Hmong: kaum ib

French: onze

e-mail (EE-mayl)

Spanish: correo electrónico

Pilipino: e-mail

Vietnamese: thư điện tử

Chinese: 电子邮件 / 電子郵件

Hmong: ntawv xa hauv hluav taws xob

French: courrier électronique

engineer (en-juh-NEER)

Spanish: ingeniero / ingeniera

Pilipino: inhinyero

Vietnamese: kỹ sư

Chinese: 工程师 / 工程師

Hmong: tus kws laj tim thawj

French: ingénieur

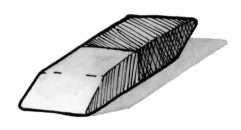

eraser (i-RAY-sur)

Spanish: borrador

Pilipino: pambura

Vietnamese: cục tẩy

Chinese: 橡皮

Hmong: lub voov xuam

French: gomme

eye (iy)

Spanish: ojo

Pilipino: mata

Vietnamese: con mắt

Chinese: 眼

Hmong: qhov muag

French: œil

46

eyebrow (IY-brow)

Spanish: ceja

Pilipino: kilay

Vietnamese: lông mày

Chinese: 眉毛

Hmong: plaub muag theem saum toj

French: sourcil

eyelash (IY-lash)

Spanish: pestaña

Pilipino: pilikmata

Vietnamese: lông mi

Chinese: 睫毛

Hmong: plaub muag

French: cil

eyelid (IY-lid)

Spanish: párpado

Pilipino: takup mata

Vietnamese: mí mắt

Chinese: 眼皮

Hmong: tawv muag

French: paupière

a b c d **e** f g h i j k l m n o p q r s t u v w x y z

F f f f

face (fays)

Spanish: cara, rostro

Vietnamese: cái mặt

Hmong: ntsej muag

Pilipino: mukha

Chinese: 脸 / 臉

French: visage

fall (fawl)

Spanish: otoño

Vietnamese: mùa thu

Hmong: lub caij nplooj ntoos zeeg

Pilipino: taglagas

Chinese: 秋

French: automne

family (FAM-uh-lee)

Spanish: familia

Vietnamese: gia đình

Hmong: tsev neeg

Pilipino: pamilya

Chinese: 家族 / 家庭

French: famille

family room (FAM-uh-lee room)

Spanish: sala de estar

Vietnamese: phòng gia đình

Hmong: chav tsev neeg nyob

Pilipino: silid pamilya

Chinese: 起居室

French: salle de séjour

fan (fan)

Spanish: ventilador

Vietnamese: cái quạt

Hmong: kiv cua

Pilipino: bentilador

Chinese: 电风扇 / 電風扇

French: ventilateur

farmer (FAHR-mur)

Spanish: granjero

Vietnamese: nông gia

Hmong: tswv teb, neeg ua liaj ua teb

Pilipino: magsasaka

Chinese: 农夫 / 農夫

French: fermière / fermier

father (FAH-<u>th</u>ur)

Spanish: padre

Vietnamese: cha

Hmong: txiv

Pilipino: ama

Chinese: 父亲 / 父親

French: père

fawn (fawn)

Spanish: cervato

Vietnamese: con hươu con

Hmong: me nyuam mos lwj

Pilipino: batang usa

Chinese: 小鹿

French: faon

February (FEB-roo-ayr-ee)

Spanish: febrero

Vietnamese: tháng hai

Hmong: lub ob hlis ntuj

Pilipino: Pebrero

Chinese: 二月

French: février

fifteen (fif-TEEN)

15

fifteen ladybugs

Spanish: quince

Vietnamese: mười lăm

Hmong: kaum tsib

Pilipino: labinlima

Chinese: 十五

French: quinze

a b c d e f g h i j k l m n o p q r s t u v w x y z

49

floor (flohr)

Spanish: piso   **Pilipino:** sahig

Vietnamese: sàn nhà   **Chinese:** 地板

Hmong: lub plag tsev   **French:** sol

flower (FLOW-ur)

Spanish: flor   **Pilipino:** bulaklak

Vietnamese: bông hoa   **Chinese:** 花

Hmong: lub paj   **French:** fleur

fly (fliy)

Spanish: mosca   **Pilipino:** langaw

Vietnamese: con ruồi   **Chinese:** 苍蝇 / 蒼蠅

Hmong: yoov   **French:** mouche

foot (fut)

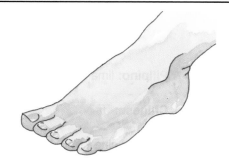

Spanish: pie   **Pilipino:** paa

Vietnamese: bàn chân   **Chinese:** 脚 / 腳

Hmong: txhais taw   **French:** pied

football (FUT-bawl)

Spanish: fútbol   **Pilipino:** putbol

Vietnamese: banh cà na   **Chinese:** 足球

Hmong: pob txawb txhom   **French:** ballon de football américain

forehead (FOHR-id)

Spanish: frente

Vietnamese: cái trán

Hmong: hauv pliaj

Pilipino: noo

Chinese: 额 / 額頭

French: front

fork (fohrk)

Spanish: tenedor

Vietnamese: cái nĩa

Hmong: diav rawg

Pilipino: tinidor

Chinese: 叉

French: fourchette

forty (FOHR-tee)

40

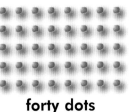

forty dots

Spanish: cuarenta

Vietnamese: bốn mươi

Hmong: plaub caug

Pilipino: apatnapu

Chinese: 四十

French: quarante

four (fohr)

4

four balloons

Spanish: cuatro

Vietnamese: bốn

Hmong: plaub

Pilipino: apat

Chinese: 四

French: quatre

fourteen (fohr-TEEN)

14

fourteen spiders

Spanish: catorce

Vietnamese: mười bốn

Hmong: kaum plaub

Pilipino: labing-apat

Chinese: 十四

French: quatorze

a b c d e **f** g h i j k l m n o p q r s t u v w x y z

Hh

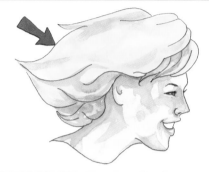

hair (hayr)

Spanish: pelo **Pilipino:** buhok

Vietnamese: tóc **Chinese:** 头发 / 頭髮

Hmong: plaub hau **French:** cheveux

hairbrush (HAYR-brush)

Spanish: cepillo para el pelo **Pilipino:** brush ng buhok

Vietnamese: bàn chải tóc **Chinese:** 发刷 / 髮刷

Hmong: zuag ntsis plaubhau **French:** brosse à chevaux

hairdresser (HAYR-dres-ur)

Spanish: peluquera / peluquero **Pilipino:** tagapag-ayos ng buhok

Vietnamese: thợ làm tóc **Chinese:** 美发师 / 美髮師

Hmong: tus kho plaubhau **French:** coiffeur

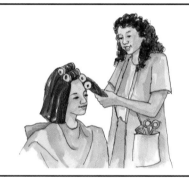

half-dollar (haf-DAHL-ur)

Spanish: medio dólar **Pilipino:** kalahating dolyar

Vietnamese: nửa mỹ kim **Chinese:** 半块钱 / 半塊錢

Hmong: lub nyiaj tsib caug xees **French:** pièce de cinquante cents

half-hour (haf-OWR)

Spanish: media hora **Pilipino:** kalahating oras

Vietnamese: nửa giờ **Chinese:** 半小时 / 半小時

Hmong: peb caug feeb **French:** demi-heure

half-past (haf-PAST)

half-past 2 o'clock

Spanish: ...y media

Pilipino: y media

Vietnamese: nửa giờ sau

Chinese: 过了半··· / 過了半···

Hmong: peb caug feeb dhau

French: et demi

ham (ham)

Spanish: jamón

Pilipino: hamon

Vietnamese: thịt đùi heo muối

Chinese: 火腿

Hmong: ib hom nqaij npuas

French: jambon

hamburger (HAM-bur-gur)

Spanish: hamburguesa

Pilipino: hamburger

Vietnamese: bánh mì hăm-bơc-gơ

Chinese: 煎牛肉饼 / 漢堡

Hmong: nqaij nyuj nrog mov mog ci

French: hamburger

hammer (HAM-ur)

Spanish: martillo

Pilipino: martilyo

Vietnamese: cái búa

Chinese: 锤 / 鎚

Hmong: rauj

French: marteau

hand (hand)

Spanish: mano

Pilipino: kamay

Vietnamese: bàn tay

Chinese: 手

Hmong: txhais tes

French: main

a b c d e f g **h** i j k l m n o p q r s t u v w x y z

61

A
B
C
D
E
F
G
H
I
J
K
L
M
N
O
P
Q
R
S
T
U
V
W
X
Y
Z

hat (hat)

Spanish: sombrero   **Pilipino:** sumbrero

Vietnamese: cái mũ   **Chinese:** 帽子

Hmong: kos mom   **French:** chapeau

head (hed)

Spanish: cabeza   **Pilipino:** ulo

Vietnamese: cái đầu   **Chinese:** 头 / 頭

Hmong: taub hau   **French:** tête

heater (HEE-tur)

Spanish: calentador   **Pilipino:** pampainit

Vietnamese: máy sưởi   **Chinese:** 暖气 / 暖氣機

Hmong: lub tso pa sov   **French:** appareil de chauffage

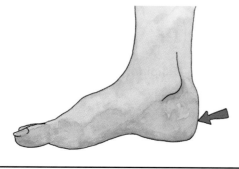

heel (heel)

Spanish: talón   **Pilipino:** sakong

Vietnamese: gót chân   **Chinese:** 后脚跟 / 後脚跟

Hmong: pob taws   **French:** talon

helicopter
(HEL-i-kahp-tur)

Spanish: helicóptero   **Pilipino:** helikopter

Vietnamese: máy bay trực thăng   **Chinese:** 直升飞机 / 直昇飛機

Hmong: dav hlaub qav taub   **French:** hélicoptère

Dictionary Detective

Hen and *horse* are animals. What is the only word in this book that is an animal that begins with the letter z?

hen (hen)

Spanish: gallina   **Pilipino:** inahin

Vietnamese: con gà mái   **Chinese:** 母鸡 / 母雞

Hmong: poj qaib   **French:** poule

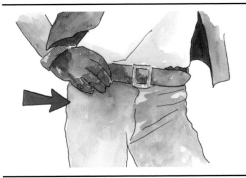

hip (hip)

Spanish: cadera   **Pilipino:** balakang

Vietnamese: cái hông   **Chinese:** 臀部

Hmong: ntshag   **French:** hanche

hippopotamus (hip-uh-PAHT-uh-mus)

Spanish: hipopótamo   **Pilipino:** hipopotamus

Vietnamese: con hà mã   **Chinese:** 河马 / 河馬

Hmong: xib nywg   **French:** hippopotame

hoe (hoh)

Spanish: azada, azadón   **Pilipino:** asarol

Vietnamese: cái cuốc   **Chinese:** 镐 / 鈀

Hmong: hlau   **French:** binette, pioche, bêche

horse (hohrs)

Spanish: caballo   **Pilipino:** kabayo

Vietnamese: con ngựa   **Chinese:** 马 / 馬

Hmong: nees   **French:** cheval

a b c d e f g **h** i j k l m n o p q r s t u v w x y z

hose (hohz)

Spanish: manguera   **Pilipino:** gomang

Vietnamese: ống nước   **Chinese:** 水管

Hmong: hlua dej   **French:** tuyau

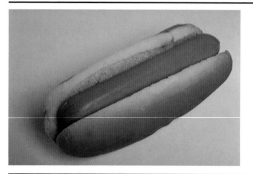

hot dog (haht dawg)

Spanish: perrito caliente   **Pilipino:** hotdog

Vietnamese: dồi hot-doóc   **Chinese:** 热狗 / 熱狗

Hmong: nyhuv txwm   **French:** hot-dog

hour (owr)

Spanish: hora   **Pilipino:** oras

Vietnamese: giờ đồng hồ   **Chinese:** 小时 / 小時

Hmong: thaus, teev   **French:** heure

hour hand

hour hand (owr hand)

Spanish: manilla de reloj, manecilla del reloj   **Pilipino:** maikling kamay ng relo

Vietnamese: kim chỉ giờ   **Chinese:** 时针 / 時針

Hmong: tus ntiag teev   **French:** petite aiguille

house (hows)

Spanish: casa   **Pilipino:** bahay

Vietnamese: nhà   **Chinese:** 房子 / 房屋

Hmong: tsev   **French:** maison

ice (iys)

Spanish: hielo

Vietnamese: nước đá

Hmong: dej khov

Pilipino: yelo

Chinese: 冰 / 冰

French: glace

ice cream (iys kreem)

Spanish: helado

Vietnamese: cà rem

Hmong: kee lees

Pilipino: sorbetes

Chinese: 冰淇淋

French: glace

ice skate (iys skayt)

Spanish: patín para hielo

Vietnamese: giày trượt băng

Hmong: caij khau log saum dej khov

Pilipino: ice skate

Chinese: 滑冰 / 滑冰

French: patin à glace

Internet (IN-tur-net)

Spanish: Internet

Vietnamese: liên mạng

Hmong: kaib tsim meej haiv

Pilipino: Internet

Chinese: 互联网 / 網際網路, 互聯網

French: Internet

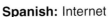

iron (IY-urn)

Spanish: plancha

Vietnamese: cái bàn ủi

Hmong: lus luam khaub ncaws

Pilipino: plantsa

Chinese: 熨斗

French: fer à repasser

moccasin
(MAHK-uh-sin)

Spanish: mocasín **Pilipino:** mokasin

Vietnamese: giày da đế bẹt **Chinese:** 平底鞋

Hmong: ib hom khau **French:** mocassin

Monday (MUHN-day)

Spanish: lunes **Pilipino:** Lunes

Vietnamese: Thứ Hai **Chinese:** 星期一

Hmong: Zwj Hli **French:** lundi

money (MUHN-ee)

Spanish: dinero **Pilipino:** pera

Vietnamese: tiền **Chinese:** 钱 / 錢, 紙幣

Hmong: nyiaj **French:** argent

monitor (MAHN-uh-tur)

Spanish: monitor **Pilipino:** monitor

Vietnamese: màn hình để theo dõi **Chinese:** 屏幕 / 電腦螢幕

Hmong: lub ntsiab thawj kaib lawj ceem **French:** moniteur

monkey (MUHN-kee)

Spanish: mono **Pilipino:** uggoy

Vietnamese: con khỉ **Chinese:** 猴

Hmong: tus liab **French:** singe

moose (moos)

Spanish: alce

Vietnamese: một loài hươu

Hmong: mos lwj ntxhuav

Pilipino: moose

Chinese: 麋鹿

French: orignal

mop (mahp)

Spanish: fregona

Vietnamese: chổi lau nhà

Hmong: tus txhuam tsev

Pilipino: mop

Chinese: 拖把

French: serpillière

mosquito (muh-SKEE-toh)

Spanish: mosquito

Vietnamese: con muỗi

Hmong: yoov tshaj cum

Pilipino: lamok

Chinese: 蚊

French: moustique

mother (MUH<u>TH</u>-ur)

Spanish: madre

Vietnamese: mẹ

Hmong: niam

Pilipino: inay

Chinese: 母亲 / 母親

French: mère

motorcycle (MOH-tur-siy-kul)

Spanish: motocicleta

Vietnamese: xe gắn máy

Hmong: tsheb nees zab

Pilipino: motorsiklo

Chinese: 机器脚踏车 / 摩托車

French: moto

A B C D E F G H I J K L M N O **P** Q R S T U V W X Y Z

plumber (PLUHM-ur)

Spanish: plomero   **Pilipino:** tubero

Vietnamese: thợ ống nước   **Chinese:** 铅工 / 鉛工

Hmong: kws kho dej   **French:** plombier

polar bear
(POH-lur bayr)

Spanish: oso polar   **Pilipino:** osong polar

Vietnamese: gấu trắng bắc cực   **Chinese:** 北极熊 / 北極熊

Hmong: dais dawb   **French:** ours blanc, ours polaire

police car
(puh-LEES kahr)

Spanish: coche de policía   **Pilipino:** kotse ng pulis

Vietnamese: xe cảnh sát   **Chinese:** 警车 / 警車

Hmong: tsheb tub ceev xwm   **French:** voiture de police

police officer
(puh-LEES AW-fi-sur)

Spanish: agente de policía   **Pilipino:** pulis

Vietnamese: cảnh sát viên   **Chinese:** 警察

Hmong: tub ceev xwm   **French:** officier de police, policier

popcorn (PAHP-kohrn)

Spanish: palomitas de maíz   **Pilipino:** papkorn

Vietnamese: bắp rang dòn   **Chinese:** 爆米花

Hmong: paj kws   **French:** pop-corn

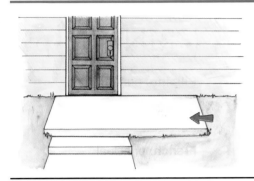

porch (pohrch)

Spanish: porche

Pilipino: portiko

Vietnamese: hiên nhà

Chinese: 门口 / 門口

Hmong: lawj (qis)

French: véranda

porcupine (POHR-kyuh-piyn)

Spanish: puerco espín

Pilipino: porkyupayn

Vietnamese: con nhím

Chinese: 豪猪

Hmong: tsaug

French: porc-épic

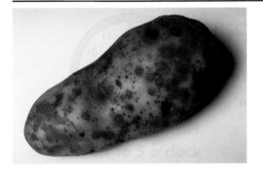

potato (puh-TAY-toh)

Spanish: patata, papa

Pilipino: patatas

Vietnamese: khoai tây

Chinese: 土豆 / 馬鈴薯

Hmong: qos yaj ywm

French: pomme de terre

potato chip (puh-TAY-toh chip)

Spanish: papas fritas

Pilipino: potato chip

Vietnamese: lát khoai tây chiên dòn

Chinese: 油炸土豆片 / 洋芋片

Hmong: qos yaj ywm kib

French: chips

president (PREZ-uh-dunt)

Spanish: presidente / presidenta

Pilipino: pangulo

Vietnamese: tổng thống

Chinese: 总统 / 總統

Hmong: thawj kav xwm haiv

French: président

a
b
c
d
e
f
g
h
i
j
k
l
m
n
o
p
q
r
s
t
u
v
w
x
y
z

Dictionary Detective

Saturday is one of the days of the week. Look at the table of contents. Which page tells you **all** the days of the week?

sandwich (SAND-wich)

Spanish: sandwich

Pilipino: sanwits

Vietnamese: bánh mì săn uých

Chinese: 三明治

Hmong: ncuav cij rau nqaib

French: sandwich

Saturday (SAT-ur-day)

Spanish: sábado

Pilipino: Sabado

Vietnamese: thứ bảy

Chinese: 星期六

Hmong: Zwj Cag

French: samedi

saw (saw)

Spanish: sierra

Pilipino: lagari

Vietnamese: cái cưa

Chinese: 锯子 / 鋸子

Hmong: kaw

French: scie

school bus (skool buhs)

Spanish: autobús escolar

Pilipino: bus na pangeskuwela

Vietnamese: xe buýt học đường

Chinese: 校车 / 校車

Hmong: tsheb thauj me nyuam kawm ntawv

French: autobus scolaire

scissors (SIZ-urz)

Spanish: tijeras

Pilipino: gunting

Vietnamese: cái kéo

Chinese: 剪刀

Hmong: rab txiab

French: ciseaux

sea (see)

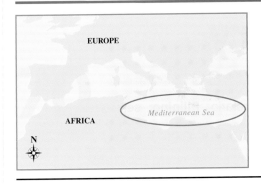

EUROPE

AFRICA

Mediterranean Sea

N

Spanish: mar

Vietnamese: biển

Hmong: dej hiav txwv

Pilipino: dagat

Chinese: 海

French: mer

sea horse (SEE hohrs)

Spanish: caballito de mar

Vietnamese: con cá ngựa

Hmong: nees dej

Pilipino: kabayong-dagat

Chinese: 海马 / 海馬

French: hippocampe

sea turtle (see TURT-ul)

Spanish: tortuga de mar

Vietnamese: con rùa biển

Hmong: vaub kib dej

Pilipino: pawikan

Chinese: 海龟 / 海龜

French: tortue de mer

seal (seel)

Spanish: foca

Vietnamese: con hải cẩu

Hmong: ntshuab

Pilipino: poka

Chinese: 海狗

French: phoque

second (SEK-und)

Spanish: segundo

Vietnamese: thứ nhì

Hmong: zus ob

Pilipino: pangalawa

Chinese: 第二

French: second

a
b
c
d
e
f
g
h
i
j
k
l
m
n
o
p
q
r
s
t
u
v
w
x
y
z

A B C D E F G H I J K L M N O P Q R **S** T U V W X Y Z

16

sixteen flies

sixteen (sik-STEEN)

Spanish: dieciséis

Vietnamese: mười sáu

Hmong: kaum rau

Pilipino: labing-anim

Chinese: 十六

French: seize

sixth (siksth)

Spanish: sexto

Vietnamese: thứ sáu

Hmong: zus rau

Pilipino: pang-anim

Chinese: 第六

French: sixième

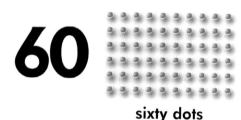

60

sixty dots

sixty (SIK-stee)

Spanish: sesenta

Vietnamese: sáu mươi

Hmong: rau caum

Pilipino: animnapu

Chinese: 六十

French: soixante

skateboard (SKAYT-bohrd)

Spanish: monopatín

Vietnamese: ván trượt

Hmong: daim ntoo log khau

Pilipino: isketbord

Chinese: 溜冰板

French: planche à roulettes

skin (skin)

Spanish: piel

Vietnamese: da

Hmong: tawv nqaij

Pilipino: balat

Chinese: 皮肤／皮膚

French: peau

skirt (skurt)

Spanish: falda

Pilipino: palda

Vietnamese: cái váy

Chinese: 裙子

Hmong: daim tiab

French: jupe

skunk (skuhnk)

Spanish: zorrillo, mofeta

Pilipino: skunk

Vietnamese: con chồn hôi

Chinese: 臭鼬鼠

Hmong: puam tsw sem

French: moufette

sky (skiy)

Spanish: cielo

Pilipino: langit

Vietnamese: bầu trời

Chinese: 天空

Hmong: saum ntuj

French: ciel

slide (sliyd)

Spanish: resbaladero

Pilipino: padulasan

Vietnamese: cầu tuột

Chinese: 滑板 / 溜滑梯

Hmong: zawv zawg

French: toboggan

slipper (SLIP-ur)

Spanish: pantufla, zapatilla

Pilipino: tsinelas

Vietnamese: dép đi trong nhà

Chinese: 拖鞋

Hmong: khau rau hauv tsev

French: pantoufle

a b c d e f g h i j k l m n o p q r s t u v w x y z

113

tricycle (TRIY-sik-ul)

Spanish: triciclo

Pilipino: traysikel

Vietnamese: xe đạp ba bánh

Chinese: 三轮脚踏车 / 三輪車

Hmong: tsheb kauj vab peb lub log

French: tricycle

truck (truk)

Spanish: camioneta, camión

Pilipino: trak

Vietnamese: xe tải

Chinese: 卡车 / 卡車

Hmong: tsheb thauj khoom

French: camionnette, camion

truck driver (truk DRIY-vur)

Spanish: camionero

Pilipino: tsuper ng trak

Vietnamese: tài xế xe tải

Chinese: 卡车驾驶员 / 卡車駕駛員

Hmong: tus neeg tsav tsheb thauj khoom

French: conducteur de camion

Tuesday (TOOZ-day)

Spanish: martes

Pilipino: Martes

Vietnamese: thứ ba

Chinese: 星期二

Hmong: Zwj Quag

French: mardi

turkey (TUR-kee)

Spanish: pavo

Pilipino: pabo

Vietnamese: gà tây

Chinese: 火鸡 / 火雞

Hmong: qaib cov txwv

French: dinde

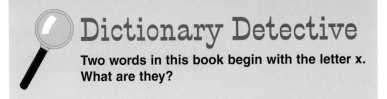
turtle (TURT-ul)

Spanish: tortuga

Vietnamese: con rùa

Hmong: vaub kib

Pilipino: pagong

Chinese: 乌龟 / 烏龜

French: tortue

twelve (twelv)

12

twelve pencils

Spanish: doce

Vietnamese: mười hai

Hmong: kaum ob

Pilipino: labindalawa

Chinese: 十二

French: douze

twenty (TWEN-tee)

20

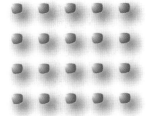

twenty dots

Spanish: veinte

Vietnamese: hai mươi

Hmong: nees nkaum

Pilipino: dalawampu

Chinese: 二十

French: vingt

two (too)

2

two cupcakes

Spanish: dos

Vietnamese: hai

Hmong: ob

Pilipino: dalawa

Chinese: 二

French: deux

typewriter (TIYP-riy-tur)

Spanish: máquina de escribir

Vietnamese: máy đánh chữ

Hmong: tshuab ntaus ntawv

Pilipino: makinilya

Chinese: 打字机 / 打字機

French: machine à écrire

a b c d e f g h i j k l m n o p q r s t u v w x y z

129

Uu

umbrella (um-BREL-uh)

Spanish: paraguas

Pilipino: payong

Vietnamese: cây dù

Chinese: 伞 / 傘

Hmong: lub kaus

French: parapluie

uncle (UNG-kul)

Spanish: tío

Pilipino: tiyo

Vietnamese: cậu, chú, bác

Chinese: 伯父,叔父,姑父,姨丈 / 伯父,叔父,姑丈,姨丈

Hmong: dab laug, txiv hlob, txiv ntxawm

French: oncle

underwear (UHN-dur-wayr)

Spanish: ropa interior

Pilipino: pang-ilalim

Vietnamese: đồ lót

Chinese: 内衣裤 / 內衣褲

Hmong: ris tshos xuab

French: sous-vêtements

A B C D E F G H I J K L M N O P Q R S T **U** V W X Y Z

130

Vv

vacuum cleaner
(VAK-yoom KLEEN-ur)

Spanish: aspiradora   **Pilipino:** bakyum

Vietnamese: máy hút bụi   **Chinese:** 吸尘器 / 吸塵器

Hmong: tshuab nqus tsev   **French:** aspirateur

van (van)

Spanish: furgoneta, camioneta   **Pilipino:** ban

Vietnamese: xe van   **Chinese:** 行理车 / 行李車

Hmong: lub tsheb loj thauj neeg   **French:** camionnette

VCR (VEE-SEE-AHR)

Spanish: VCR   **Pilipino:** VCR

Vietnamese: máy chiếu video   **Chinese:** 录像机 / 錄影機

Hmong: lub tshuab VCR   **French:** magnétoscope

veterinarian
(vet-ur-uh-NAYR-ee-uhn)

Spanish: veterinario / veterinaria   **Pilipino:** beterinaryo

Vietnamese: bác sĩ thú y   **Chinese:** 兽医 / 獸醫

Hmong: kws kho tsiaj mob   **French:** vétérinaire

videotape
(VID-ee-oh-tayp)

Spanish: cinta de vídeo   **Pilipino:** bidyo

Vietnamese: băng video   **Chinese:** 录像带 / 錄影帶

Hmong: roj hmab yees duab   **French:** vidéocassette

a b c d e f g h i j k l m n o p q r s t u **v** w x y z

worm (wurm)

Spanish: gusano   **Pilipino:** bulati

Vietnamese: con sâu, con trùn   **Chinese:** 虫／蟲

Hmong: cua nab   **French:** ver

wrist (rist)

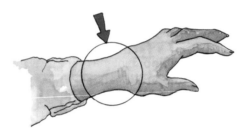

Spanish: muñeca   **Pilipino:** pulsuhan

Vietnamese: cổ tay   **Chinese:** 手腕

Hmong: dab teg   **French:** poignet

A B C D E F G H I J K L M N O P Q R S T U V **W** X Y Z

136

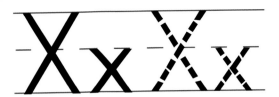

x-ray (EKS-ray)

Spanish: radiografía   **Pilipino:** x-ray

Vietnamese: chiếu điện, phim chiếu điện   **Chinese:** X射线 / X光線

Hmong: ntsuas hluav taws xob   **French:** rayon X

xylophone
(ZIY-luh-fohn)

Spanish: xilófono   **Pilipino:** saylopon

Vietnamese: đàn gõ   **Chinese:** 木琴

Hmong: lub tshuab ntaus nkauj hu xylophone   **French:** xylophone

a
b
c
d
e
f
g
h
i
j
k
l
m
n
o
p
q
r
s
t
u
v
w
x
y
z

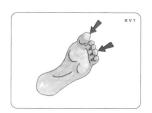

Introduce sounds in context. Introduce the sounds of the English language in context and provide examples of words that have those sounds. For example, /t/ is what we hear at the beginning of *toes*, *trumpet*, and *tiger*. Encourage students to make dictionaries, create word walls, use egg cartons to house pictures and/or words with similar elements, or make scrapbooks of pictures and words. This will help students understand how to apply the sounds. These activities also reinforce the connection between sounds and the letters that represent them.

▲ *Readers need exposure to words in many settings such as word cards, practice pages, and readers.*

Encourage students to write. Reading and writing are different sides of the same literacy coin. Students who write as they learn phonics tend to read faster and better than those who do not. This is especially true when students are encouraged to utilize personalized spelling for words that may not be part of their writing vocabulary. For example, writers who are willing to attempt to spell *tight* by producing *tite* or *tiet* are more likely to succeed in phonics than those who are reluctant to take such risks. Practice in producing the written form of words is an excellent way to both apply multisensory practice and demonstrate the relationship between sounds and the letters that represent them.

▲ *Give students many opportunities to write. The student work above comes from an IDEAS for Literature student journal.*

Consider the student's native language. Students who are not native English speakers may encounter great difficulties with English. This is particularly true for students whose native language is not alphabetic (e.g., Chinese) or whose language is very phonetic (e.g., Spanish). Teachers need to focus on key phonics components and provide opportunities for English learners to practice seeing and hearing the sounds and letters. Moving too quickly from one new sound to another will confuse students and interfere with the mastery necessary to learn the elements. Provide visuals, such as *IDEA Picture & Word* cards, as well as actions to solidify a concept or word meaning and to make sure students hear and see the target words. You can help learners make the connections between ideas and words. Begin with pictures of simple, concrete words (e.g., *cat*, *house*, *tree*) and then move to more abstract ones (e.g., *government*, *helpers*, *structure*).

Activities to Strengthen Dictionary Skills

* 1, 2, 3, GO! Have each student place their closed dictionary on their desk. Tell students that you will give them a word and they are going to race to see who will be the first to find the word in the dictionary. Pick a word from the dictionary (e.g., pig) and say "Pig. One, Two, Three, GO!" The student who finds the word first, must raise their hand. After you call on the student, ask him or her to tell you the page on which he or she found the word and the first letter of the word. Then, that student will get to choose a word and lead the class in another round of 1, 2, 3, GO!

* Six Degrees of Separation Word Web. On the board, write a word from the dictionary (e.g., lamb) and ask students to find it in their dictionaries. Then, ask students to think of as many other words in the dictionary that might describe lamb (e.g., white, baby animal, sheep) as they can think of. Ask students to look up those words in the dictionary and continue to think of other words in the dictionary that relate to those new words. Write them on the board in a word web, as shown below. Keep going until students run out of ideas, or as long as time permits.

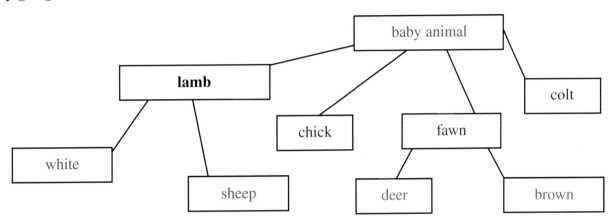

* What Am I? Pick a word from the dictionary. Tell students that they are going to have to ask you "yes" and "no" questions in order to figure out what you are. Make sure they keep their dictionaries handy, so they can look up clues. For example, let's say you have chosen "mother." Students may ask questions such as "Are you a food? Are you a person? Are you male? Are you female? Are you an occupation? Are you a family member? Do you start with the letter 'm'? Are you 'mother'?" and so forth. Make sure students know that they are to raise their hands before shouting out questions or guesses. The student who guesses correctly gets to lead the class in another round of What am I?

* It Starts With A "C"! Divide the class into groups of two. Think of a category (such as animals, people, household items, and so forth). Ask student groups to write all the English words they can think of in that category that begin with the letter "c." Give them a set amount of time to complete this activity. Afterwards, count how many words each group came up with. Continue playing by giving students a new category and a new letter of the alphabet.

Animals that start with a "C":	
calf	cow
chick	caterpillar
colt	cat
camel	chipmunk
chicken	

* **My "Top Ten" Picture Dictionary.** Ask students to make a list of their 10 favorite foods, singers, books, songs, television shows, or whatever else you decide. Then tell them that they are going to make their own very own "Top Ten" Picture Dictionary. Have them begin by writing each word on its own separate page, so their dictionaries will be ten pages long. Have them place their words in alphabetical order. Then, have them write a phonetic spelling of the words, the number of syllables each word has in it, and, if possible, the words in their native language. Then have them complete the activity by drawing a picture to go with the word. They can also create and decorate a cover page for their "Top Ten" Picture Dictionary!

* **How Many Syllables Do You Hear?** Have students cut a piece of paper into three pieces. Ask them to write the numeral 1 on the first sheet, the numeral 2 on the second sheet, and the numeral 3 on the third sheet. Slowly call out vocabulary words from the dictionary and have students hold up the paper with the corresponding number of syllables. If students are having trouble understanding the concept of syllables, review "Here's the Key!" with them on pages 6-7, or allow them to look up the words in the dictionary.

* **Picture This!** Divide the class into two teams. Give a student from Team One a word from the *IDEA Picture Dictionary 1*. The student's goal is to draw a picture of that word so that the student's team can guess it. Give Team One a minute to guess the correct word. If the team guesses correctly, it wins five points. If not, Team Two gets a chance to guess and wins the five points if the answer is correct. Then a student from Team Two gets a new dictionary word and draws a picture for Team Two to guess.